DADisms

DADisms

WHAT HE SAYS AND WHAT HE REALLY MEANS

by Cathy Hamilton

**Andrews McMeel
Publishing**

Kansas City

ISBN-13: 978-0-7407-2288-2
ISBN-10: 0-7407-2288-3

Library of Congress Control Number: 2001095910

Book design by Holly Camerlinck

Attention: Schools and Businesses

Andrews McMeel books are available at quantity discounts with bulk purchase for educational, business, or sales promotional use. For information, please write to: Special Sales Department, Andrews McMeel Publishing, LLC, an Andrews McMeel Universal company, 4520 Main Street, Kansas City, Missouri 64111.

To Rex and Tom—two of the best
dads in the whole wide world.

"When I was your age . . ."

{ One of the most common isms, it's frequently followed by one of the following big fat lies: }

I **walked** to school ten miles in the snow, uphill both ways!

They didn't have indoor plumbing. We had to go **outside** to do our business.

Kids didn't **speak** until they were spoken to.

Men were kings of the castle and women **knew their place**.

We were **so poor**, we ate dirt . . . and were glad to have it.

I treated **my** father with respect.

"They don't make 'em like that anymore."

{ Usually used in reference to cars, houses, movies, and women, this is the classic father's lament. }

Translation:

"It's **hell** getting old."

"Turn that racket down! I can't hear myself think!"

Racket (n): Music, of any genre, played by the younger generation at decibels exceeding the volume of the television Dad is watching, particularly when *Monday Night Football* is on.

3

"If you fall and break your leg, don't come running to me."

Translation:

"Be **careful** up there. Our health insurance policy has a $200 deductible."

"That's the best way I know to put out an eye!"

{ Dad is being sarcastic here. What he means is, "Don't run with that stick!" }

5

(Dads love sarcasm. It's a great way to express their concern but still act tough.)

"A penny saved is a penny earned."

{ This Ben Franklin gem has been repeated by dads for generations, though the logic is lost on most kids in the twenty-first century, half of whom don't know what a penny is. }

"Look it up in the dictionary."

{ This dadism is used to foster educational self-sufficiency, resourcefulness, and initiative. }

Translation:

7

"Are you nuts? I have no idea how to spell **pneumonia** and I'm too damned old to learn!"

"It's not whether you win or lose, it's how you play the game."

{
Frequently offered as words of condolence to a child who has just suffered an agonizing defeat, this dadism is usually followed by an invitation to go out for ice cream or a beer, depending on the kid's age.
}

8

"You better not let your mom hear you saying that."

Translation:

"I'm too tired to discipline you
for a small infraction like a CUSS word,
especially since you probably
learned that word from me. Just don't
try it in front of your *mother* or we'll
both be sorry!"

"This is going to hurt me a lot more than it hurts you."

This strange, guilt-ridden disclaimer is commonly used before a dad inflicts punishment on a child. The intended translation: "Even as I'm swatting your behind or taking away your car keys, I'm suffering more than you can possibly know."

Kids never believe this for a second.

"Close your mouth and eat your supper."

{ Taken literally, of course, this dadism is an impossible feat. }

Translation:

"Stop talking and finish your food before it gets cold. That steak cost me **four** bucks a pound."

"After the game."

{
Children, wives, or innocent bystanders who
are naive enough to make requests of a dad
who is busy watching a sporting event on TV
from the comfort of his recliner are guaranteed to hear this retort.
}

"No pain, no gain."

A somewhat feeble attempt at motivational speaking, this one is used to inspire a child to run one more lap, lift one more bushel, or endure one more round of multiplication tables.

Kids really hate this one.

"Rise and shine!"

(Alternate isms: "The early bird gets the worm," "Up 'n' at 'em!," "Wake up, little Susie," "Hey, Sleepyhead . . . time to get shakin'.")

14

Dads take sadistic pleasure in rousing the rest of their families from bed early in the morning. Perhaps Dad figures if he has to get up at the crack of dawn to go out and earn a living, the rest of the family should share in the misery. Some dads use this morning ritual to play motivational speaker.

Sometimes, even moms hate this one.

"They're just jealous, that's all."

An honorable but often futile attempt to comfort a child who has been treated cruelly by his or her peers.

This dadism is often uttered through clenched teeth as Dad plans the slow and painful death of his kid's tormenters.

"Look at me when I'm talking to you."

Most dads are under the misguided impression that they have their kids' full attention when they have achieved eye contact. That's why many dads insist that the child actually meet their gaze when getting a good tongue lashing.

16

"This'll put hair on your chest."

For reasons incomprehensible to most women, men enjoy challenging other men—especially their sons—to push the limits of good sense and/or good taste and consume extremely spicy foods or disgusting amounts of liquor.

17

Note:

There is no scientific correlation between Tabasco sauce or tequila shots and the growth of chest hair.

"Why buy the cow when you can get the milk for free?"

{ A timeless standard, this dadism carries a double meaning, even today. }

Translation:

For SONS—"What's the rush to get married if you're **already** getting lucky?"

For daughters—"Give it away too soon and you'll **never** get the guy to the altar."

"Things like this build character."

{ Used when Dad can find no other words to ease the pain of a child's broken heart or spirit, all this dadism does is make Dad feel better about the whole thing. }

"Two wrongs don't make a right."

{ This ancient adage is applied when a child has lied to cover up another misdeed such as shoplifting, sneaking a cigarette, or snarfing the last piece of Dad's birthday cake. }

"Do what I say, not what I do."

{ This common disclaimer is frequently used when a dad is not practicing what he preaches. }

Examples:

21

drinking or eating **too** much

leaving his *dirty* underwear on the **floor**

screaming

cussing

not wearing a seatbelt

wandering out in the yard in his **underwear**

"Life isn't fair."

This is the standard retort to the child's complaint: "No fair!"

Most dads will leave it at that simple, three-word reply, but, on occasion, the provoked dad will unleash a litany of woe at the unsuspecting child, such as:

22

"Fair? You think male pattern baldness is fair? Or how about that rusty heap I take to work every day? Is it fair I should still have to drive that thing while Thompson down the street gets a new SUV? Is it fair old man Simpson gave my promotion to that suck-up Wagstaff, even though I have seven years' more seniority? Is it fair that your mother gets to watch the Home and Garden channel whenever she wants, even during *Monday Night Football*? Is that fair? Huh?"

(When this happens, kids would be well
advised to quietly sneak out of the room. A
rant like this could go on for days.)

"Keep your eye on the ball."

{ A dad's quick fix to all sports-related per-
formance problems. }

(Can be modified for nonball
sports: keep your eye on the puck,
shuttlecock, etc.)

24

"Did I ever tell you about the time ..."

{ The classic prologue to Dad's tired old stories of hardship, camaraderie, brushes with death, embarrassing moments, and, sometimes, romantic encounters. }

25

Note:

It does no good to say, "Yeah, Dad, you already told us that one." You're going to hear the story again. Just sit back and go with it.

"It's time to separate the men from the boys."

This ism strikes fear into the heart of any young man who hears it. Usually, it means a boy is going to be forced to attempt something he's physically unprepared to do—a tackle football game, hunting trip, double-black diamond ski run, white water rafting, rock climbing, or going on a blind date with the boss's daughter.

"You think money grows on trees?"

{ This rhetorical question is actually more of a lament since most dads wish money *did* grow on trees. Maybe then it wouldn't be so damned hard to get the kids to rake the yard. }

"You can do anything if you just set your mind to it."

{ Another way of saying "anything's possible if you just apply yourself," this dadism seems to deny the notion of human limitations. }

28

Most kids eat this up until the age
of fourteen or so, when they figure
out that only one in approximately
14 million people actually make it to
the Olympics and even fewer grow
up to be president.

"Stand up and take it like a man."

When a dad is in the midst of a good old-fashioned, red-faced, veins-popping-through-the-neck, wild-eyed tongue lashing, the last thing he wants to see is his son slouching in a chair staring at his feet,

29

The message here is: "I may be calling you a good-for-nothing lousy slacker, but I want you to stand proud while you get your licks."

"Whatever happened to 'Respect your elders'?"

{ Symptomatic of the so-called Rodney Dangerfield syndrome, dads say this when they feel like they "get no respect," which is approximately 94 percent of the time. }

"Anything worth doing is worth doing right."

Used to promote perfection, especially when it comes to waxing the car, painting the house, or cleaning the garage, the "worth doing right" part defies argument. It's the "worth doing" part that kids will argue about.

31

"You think I was born yesterday?"

{ Kids are always trying to pull one over on the old man. Nine times out of ten, they succeed. But when Dad gets lucky and foils a youngster's scam, whatever it might be, he enjoys using this smug "gotcha": "You think I was born yesterday?" }

32

Most kids simply shake their heads and say, "You got us there, Dad," then run off to plan the next caper.

"You make a better door than a window."

{ This is Dad being subtle. }

Translation:

"You are standing in *front* of the TV. I cannot see the game. Please move to another side of the **room** so that I might have a **clear** view. You have approximately seven seconds before I start screaming."

"Walk it off."

Dad's all-purpose remedy for any sports-related injury to the hip, leg, or foot area, basically anything below the waist—fastball to the shin, bowling ball dropped on the toes, knee to the groin—this dadism is tried and true, nine times out of ten ... even though it flies in the face of conventional medical wisdom.

34

"Shake it off."

{ Same principle as "Walk it off." Applies to injuries above the waist, including head trauma. }

"Laugh it off." / "Let it roll off."

{ This is Dad's all-purpose fix for injuries to the ego or heart, such as broken dates, stinging insults, or not making the cut for a team. }

36

It rarely works but, hey,
Dad's trying!

"Never spend more than half the money you have in your pocket."

This sage advice is a good rule of thumb for everyone, although most dads tend to forget it the moment they walk into a casino or Patagonia store.

"It's just as easy to fall in love with a rich woman as it is to fall for a poor one."

{ This one speaks to most men's fantasies of falling in love with an heiress, living off her trust fund for the rest of their lives, and not having to work day in and day out for a thankless boss, paltry pay, and ten vacation days per year. }

Since most men do not achieve this dream for themselves, they extend the fantasy to their sons . . . and they to their sons . . . and so on . . . and so on . . .

"Don't ever let me catch you doing that again."

Some would argue this classic dadism sends a mixed message, which is: You can *do* it—I just don't want to *find out* about it.

The underlying principle here is: What dad doesn't know won't hurt you.

39

"I pay the cost to be the boss."

{ Since the majority of dads are not the boss in their working lives, they take great pleasure in being the boss at home. The "cost" in this case means: }

40

a) bearing the financial **burden** of providing for the household or

b) having to put up with **Mom**.

"We're making good time."

Whenever a dad (or any man, for that matter) climbs behind the wheel, he becomes hopelessly engaged in a game of Beat the Clock. Whether it's a cross-country journey or a hop across town, Dad's immediate and all-consuming goal is to make "good time."

"Good time" is a subjective term that usually means "faster than last time."

A dad will go to any lengths to make good time. That includes restricting family rest stop breaks to two minutes, exceeding speed limits by upward of twenty miles per hour, and purchasing exorbitantly expensive radar detectors to avoid getting stopped by the highway patrol. (It's not the speeding ticket Dad fears, it's the accompanying ten-minute delay.)

"Don't make me stop this car!"

In the odyssey that is the family vacation, this dadism should be considered a last-resort ultimatum. It's the red flag that should alert the family that Dad is nearing his breaking point. Should he actually have to stop the car, God forbid, all hell will break loose on the interstate.

Note:

Rarely will a dad actually pull over and stop the car because that would jeopardize his "good time," delay arrival at his destination, and forfeit his bragging rights until next year's vacation. ("Yessir, this year we made it in seven hours flat. Last year, it was 7:48. Must be that new radar detector.")

"This is just a speed bump on the journey of life."

{
Dads love using metaphors to wax poetic about life's struggles and challenges.

This one reflects Dad's ongoing obsession with making "good time."
}

"Now you listen to me, Buster (or Missy!)"

When a dad calls a son "Buster" or a daughter "Missy" the child should immediately recognize that he or she is in deep doo-doo and act accordingly.

The same applies when Dad addresses the child by his or her full name.

44

"Don't make me come in there!"

Translation:

"I don't know what you're doing behind that door. And I don't **want** to know. But if I keep hearing anymore of that God-forsaken whining, I'm going to have to get up off this couch. And if, by doing so, I miss out on the biggest play of the season, there will be **hell** to pay, Buster (or Missy)!"

45

"A little dirt never hurt anybody."

{ Like a badge of honor, dirt on the hands or clothes is a sign of a job well done or a game played hard. The dirtier a kid looks after a football game or day in the yard, the better. It doesn't matter how the dirt got there. }

This is why football players who spend more time on the bench than on the field will roll around in the dirt before heading home after a game.

"It's only a little blood. Besides, chicks dig scars."

Even better than dirt, blood is the red badge of courage—especially if you have to take a beating to get it. Young boys who come home with blood on their shirts tend to get bigger portions at dinner, more hugs, and a little extra TV time.

Part two of this dadism implies that big boys with scars get a lot more than dinner and a few hugs.

"A little pain never hurt anybody."

{ This oxymoronic statement is another twist on "Things like this build character," "Shake it off," or "No pain, no gain." }

"Turn off those lights. Do you think I'm made of money?"

{ Dads hate paying bills. They hate paying utility companies even more. }

That's why there is nothing more aggravating to a dad than lights left on in unoccupied rooms. Nothing.

"Don't give me any of your lip, young lady (man)!"

Lip *(n)*: A euphemism for talking back, usually in a raised tone of voice. Teenagers love lip but are not allowed to use it.

Dads are the only ones entitled to use lip. Lip is reserved for booing a referee's bad call, mouthing off to the next car in traffic, or talking back to the TV.

"We're not lost. I know exactly where I am."

Translation:

"I have **absolutely** no doubt that we're exactly somewhere between **home** and our destination. That's all **you** need to know!"

51

Note:

Lost is not a word that exists in any dad's vocabulary. In fact, most dads will go to extraordinary lengths to prove they are not, in fact, lost but just taking the "scenic route." All children should be taught, at as early an age as possible, never to ask dad, "Are we lost?" Women learn this shortly after taking the wedding vows, but children, whose little brains are not yet fully developed, cannot comprehend the consequences of asking this seemingly innocent question.

"Go ask your mother."

This common response is usually reserved for those sensitive questions children ask about sex or other bodily functions. It can also be used when the dad is too preoccupied by the NBA playoffs to deal with the question.

"Don't use that tone with me, young lady (man)!"

This ism stems from every dad's belief that he is the only one in the household entitled to use an authoritative tone of voice. It is "tone" that gives Dad his superior strength and power. It is exclusively his. To lose tone would be to lose everything.

53

"What are we doing— cooling the whole neighborhood?"

Worse than leaving a light on in an unoccupied room, leaving an exterior door open during extreme heat constitutes an unforgivable offense. Again, Dad's annoyance with paying the utility companies comes through loud and clear.

54

"Paying those bastards for the privilege of conditioned air is bad enough . . . but don't even think about letting that air escape!"

"Measure twice, cut once."

{ This classic ditty is *the* rule of thumb for all
do-it-yourselfers. }

It is guaranteed that all men will
ignore this advice at least once,
resulting in wasted lumber,
too-small carpet remnants, and
excess wallpaper scraps.

"Be good—but if you can't be good, be careful."

{
The ultimate parental loophole, this ism acknowledges that kids will occasionally succumb to temptation and do something they shouldn't do. Blatantly hypocritical, this dadism can be modified to apply to various situations:
}

56

Don't **drive** too **fast!** (But if you **do**, don't get a **ticket!**)

Don't have **sex!** (But if you do, use **protection!**)

Don't **drink!** (But if you **do**, don't **drive!**)

Don't do **drugs!** (But if you do, don't get **arrested!**)

"Is that what they're teaching you in school these days?"

This is Dad's pat retort to a child who disagrees with his opinion on politics, religion, or who's going to win the Super Bowl.

"Do your homework."

{ During the school year, the following exchange between father and child occurs approximately 1,345,977 times a night in the United States alone: }

58

Dad: Do your homework.

Child: I don't have any.

Dad: You've **gotta** have homework. You're in high school, for cryin' out loud!

Child: I **told** you, I don't.

Dad: Then go read a book.

Child: **Can't.** I gotta watch *Politically Incorrect* for my government class.

Dad: Is that what they're teaching you in school these days?

"Don't you know any normal boys?"

Dad's definition of *normal*: Clean, well dressed, gainfully employed, and college bound. Preferably the daughter's age but no more than two years older. Short, conservative hairstyle. No piercings or tattoos. Absent of leather except for letter jackets. Drives a conservative car. Well mannered. Comes to the front door on dates, converses with Dad with a well-rounded knowledge of business and sports, especially golf.

59

This effectively eliminates 96 percent of all teenage boys.

"As long as you live under my roof, you'll live by my rules."

{ A man's home is his castle, the only place he can truly feel like a king—at least, when Mom isn't around. And no matter how old a child may get, Dad still gets to make the rules for all who dwell under his roof. }

That is why most kids tend to leave home around the age of eighteen.

"I paid good money for that."

Good money *(n)*: Money that has been earned, inherited, won in a poker game, refunded by the IRS, etc.

61

Not to be confused with
"bad money" since, to a dad,
there's no such thing.

"Never buy the extended warranty."

{ When dads are making a major purchase, they hate paying extra money for anything— sales tax, handling fees, service contracts, and, especially, extended warranties. }

It's just the principle of the thing.

"What part of *no* don't you understand?"

{ Every day, all over the world, dads and their kids engage in the following kind of exchange: }

Kid: Dad, can I go to the Ruptured Spleen concert tonight?

Dad: No.

Kid: But **everybody's** going!

Dad: No.

Kid: But I've **already** bought tickets for fifty-five dollars **each!**

Dad: No.

Kid: I've got a **date** and a ride and **everything!**

Dad: What part of *no* don't you understand?

63

"Is that a threat or a promise? . . . Don't let the door hit you in the rear . . . I'll help you pack . . . Write when you get work!"

64

Little Sally has just thrown the tantrum of the decade. She stomps to her room, slams the door, and screams, "I'm running away from home and I'm never coming back!" That's when Dad launches into "reverse psychology" mode, all the while hoping the plan doesn't backfire because he just can't take another dramatic scene at the bus stop.

"I never talked to *my* old man like that!"

Translation:

"I can't think of a **snappy** comeback right now, so I'm going to play the guilt card. After all, it works for **Mom.**"

"Where were you raised, in a barn? It's freezing in here."

{ Dad's attempt at metaphor is usually lost on the child who absentmindedly leaves the door open on a cold day. The more effective alternative might be: }

66

Close the damn door!

"Don't take any wooden nickels!"

Translation:
"Don't get conned."

{ This dadism has been passed down through the generations, even though most dads have never seen a wooden nickel or even know what one is. }

"What do you think I am, a bank?"

{
A dad's job is to make money so he can help provide for his family. A child's job is to obtain as much of that money as possible.
}

That's why dads often feel like nothing more than an automatic bank teller . . . programmed to make nothing but withdrawals.

"You have enough money?"

Dad might complain about how kids are a constant drain on his wallet, but he'll be damned if any kid of his leaves the house with nothing in his pocket. That's why dads often slip twenty-dollar bills into their kids' hands before they go out for a night on the town.

69

And why they yell, "Be sure to bring me the change!"

"Because I said so, that's why!"

{ The difference between dads and moms is illustrated by the following examples: }

Mother and child are standing in line at the grocery store.

70

Child: Mommy, can I get some **candy?**

Mom: No.

Child: Why?

Mom: Because it's bad for your **teeth.**

Child (getting **louder**): But whyyyyy?

Mom: Because sugar causes tooth decay.

Child (**agitated** now): But whyyyyyyyyy?

Mom: Because it turns to plaque, which eats into the enamel.

Child   (in **full** whine mode): But whyyyyyyyyyy?

Mom: Because plaque, when left unchecked, creates **bacteria,** which contains **acid** that eats into the tooth's hard surface.

Child   (**breaking** the sound barrier now): But whyyyyyyyyyyyyy?

And now, the father-child scenario:

71

Child: Daddy, can I get some **candy?**

Dad: No.

Child: **Why?**

Dad: Because I **said** so, that's why!"

"Don't do anything I wouldn't do."

{ Uttered in a cautionary tone as a teenager heads out the door for the evening, this dadism implores the kid to be on his best behavior. }

Note:

Dads should resist the temptation to punctuate this ism with a sly wink of the eye. This just throws the kid into a state of confusion.

"Stop crying—or I'll really give you something to cry about!"

{ Fathers hate to hear their children cry. It breaks their hearts and makes them feel terrible. That's why dads will do just about anything to stop the tears from flowing. }

Even threaten bodily harm.

"Don't forget to call your mother. She worries about you."

{ It's a well-kept secret that dads worry just as much as moms. Of course, they'll never admit it. That's why this dadism uses Mom as a scapegoat. }

74

Dads and moms find this one
very effective.

"You're not going out in that, are you?"

{ The typical dad doesn't pay much attention to things like wardrobe. (After all, this is the man who goes for the morning paper in his Tweety Bird boxers.) But when a teenage daughter waltzes down the stairs in a miniskirt and tube top, Dad turns into the fashion gestapo. }

Note:

Short of a full suit of armor or nun's habit, no outfit will ever be sanctioned by dad for his teenage daughter.

"Get a haircut, or I'll cut it for you."

{ If there is a surefire way to motivate a son to get his hair cut, it's Dad threatening to cut it himself. }

76

This one always works.

"Hold the light steady."

{ When a dad asks a child to help him perform a bit of home or auto repair, it always means, "Hold the light." }

"Get your head out of the fridge before your ears get frostbite."

In keeping with Dad's aversion to paying money to utility companies, this ism attempts to combat the annoying habit of kids who stand for hours at a time, staring blankly at the open refrigerator, as if the food will just magically appear and prepare itself for eating.

78

"You throw like a girl."

{ There is no comment more stinging, more insulting, more self-esteem-shattering to a young athlete than "you throw like a girl." This dadism cuts to the quick. }

Even girls don't want to throw
like girls.

"You want something to do? I'll give you something to do."

{ One of the first things a child must learn is never to approach Dad on a Saturday afternoon and complain that there's nothing to do. Chances are, Dad has a list of "honey do's" in his pocket a mile long and he's just waiting for the opportunity to share the joy. }

"Check your oil."

{ As far as Dad's concerned, you can never check your oil too many times when you're away from home. }

Same holds true for the tires.

"This is your last warning."

Every dad has his own warning threshold—the number of times he gives an order before it is carried out. Some dads will ask only once and expect it to be done. Others will be content to ask twice, thrice, even five times before he runs out of patience. But when a dad says, "This is your last warning," you should take it as a serious threat.

"I'm not sleeping, I was just resting my eyes."

{ A defensive move, this ism is used when Dad gets busted sneaking a nap on the couch while watching TV. }

Note:

The only surefire way to wake a sleeping dad is to change the channel.

"Go ahead, I'll catch you."

There comes a time in every child's life when she has to take a leap of faith and jump into Dad's arms—from the side of the pool, the high bar of a swing set, or the top of a garden wall. Reassured by Dad's confident words, the child lets go and trusts that Dad will be there with open arms and an unfailing grasp. And he is there.

Then there are those smart-aleck dads who pretend to drop the poor kid within inches of the ground.

84

And we wonder why so many people are in therapy.

"What's so funny? Wipe that smile off your face."

Heaven help the poor child who dares to laugh while he's being scolded!

There is nothing more maddening to an already angry dad than a child getting the giggles during a tongue lashing. This is to be avoided at all costs, lest the child receive the full wrath of dad.

"Don't roll those eyes at me."

{ Dads don't appreciate being mocked. Especially by a gum-chewing, pink-haired, tenth-grade girl with three rings in her nose. }

After all, a guy has his limits.

"So you think you're smart, do you?"

{ What he means: "I knew my kid would be smarter than me someday. I just didn't expect that day to come so soon!" }

"Go tell your mother she wants you."

Translation:

88

"I have had just about enough of **you** for the day. Now it's your **mother's** turn. Do not come back in this room until I consume this **six-pack** and fall asleep on the couch."

"What did I just get finished telling you?"

This isn't Dad checking to see if his child is paying attention.

This is Dad forgetting what he just said and asking for an instant replay.

"If Jessie* jumped off a bridge, would you?"

{ This theoretical question is Dad's attempt to thwart peer pressure—and get himself off the hook. Usually used to rebuff typical kid arguments like: }

90

But **Jessie** gets to stay out all night!

But Jessie has a **motorcycle!**

But Jessie's **dad** let him shave his head!

But **Jessie** got his nipples **pierced!**

*Substitute any first name.

"You're only young once."

Translation:

"Live it up while you can. Because soon you'll be my age, drinking a beer in an old ratty recliner, saying things like 'You're only young once.'"

91

"You didn't beat me. I let you win."

Dads love to let their little kids beat them in cards, arm wrestling, and basketball games in the driveway. It helps build confidence and self-esteem. And, besides, it's the fatherly thing to do.

But when little kids become big kids, able to beat the old man fair and square, Dad's attitude changes, and suddenly it's every man for himself. Dad uses the above ism to save face when he inevitably loses.

No one ever believes him.

"If I've told you once, I've told you a thousand times."

{ This is Dad exaggerating. It was probably only a hundred times. }

"If I catch you doing that one more time, I'll . . ."

{ Dad makes a lot of idle threats. This is one of the more idle ones—as long as he never completes the sentence. }

"Pull my finger."

As disgusting as this fatherly ritual is, when a dad is in "pull my finger" mode, refusing to cooperate is futile. There's a sense of urgency in the "pull my finger" request. Dads tend to be very insistent ("Pull my finger. Go ahead, pull it! Hurry!") until you relent.

The tasteless payoff will give Mom fits . . . but then, who are we to deprive the old man of a bit of joy once in a while?

"Nobody said it was going to be easy."

What he says:

"Sure it's hard. The harder the better. It wasn't easy for me or my old man and I'll be damned if it's gonna be easy for you."

What he really means:

"If I could make it easier for you, I would."

"You're always gonna be my little girl."

{ A sure bet to bring a tear to a daughter's eye, this ism is reserved for special occasions like her first date, prom night, leaving home for college, and the wedding processional. }

"I love you, kid."

(No translation needed.)